Fifty
Sheds
Damper

Fifty Sheds Damper

C.T. Grey

BOXTREE

First published 2013 by Boxtree
an imprint of Pan Macmillan, a division of Macmillan Publishers Limited
Pan Macmillan, 20 New Wharf Road, London N1 9RR
Basingstoke and Oxford
Associated companies throughout the world
www.panmacmillan.com

ISBN 978-0-7522-6551-3

1 3 5 7 9 8 6 4 2

A CIP catalogue record for this book is available from the British Library.

Designed and set by seagulls.net
Printed and bound in China

Visit **www.panmacmillan.com** to read more about all our books and to buy
them. You will also find features, author interviews and news of any author
events, and you can sign up for e-newsletters so that you're always first to
hear about our new releases.

To E.L. James and A.F. Titchmarsh
– for the inspiration and the vegetation.

My chest pounds hard as my wrists strain against the cold, tight, steel handcuffs behind my back. I try to yell for help but my mouth is covered. My life flashes before my eyes – or it would do if I hadn't been blindfolded.

Questions whir round my head like a 1600-watt Qualcast rotary mower. Where am I? Who am I? Who brought me here? Robbed of my eyesight, my other senses shift into overdrive. I can feel thick, coarse rope binding my chest, waist and ankles to a wooden chair. And a tap on my forehead. Then another. Liquid splashing down onto my face. Am I being waterboarded?

Something sticky and sweet coats my tongue. Have I been drugged? That would explain my memory loss.

My twitching nostrils detect a musty, damp aroma. With just a hint of . . . what is that? It's strangely familiar but I can't place it.

Any small noise might help me discover my location but I hear nothing. I'm alone – for now. Surely not for long though. I have to get out of here before my kidnapper returns, but how?

shuffle impatiently and feel the chair move very slightly. That's it! If I can tip it back far enough to make it fall over, maybe one of its legs will break off, then I can slip free and make a run for it. I push down on the floor with the soles of my shoes. The chair moves backwards slightly before falling slowly forward again. I push harder. It moves a little further this time but once again falls stubbornly back to its starting position. I pause for a moment, take a deep breath, then kick down with all the force my aching legs can muster. I brace myself for the impact as the chair begins to rock.

And rock.

And rock.

Bugger. It's a rocking chair.

It's no use – I'm trapped, with no hope of escape. My pulse is racing, my breaths are shallow. I need to calm down. I need help. I need a nice cup of tea. But why would anyone want to kidnap me? If only I could remember who I am.

Suddenly an image flashes across my mind. A door. With a gleaming brass plate. Letters etched into it, slowly coming into focus . . .

Of course! I'm Colin T. Grey, CEO, Slea-Z-Sheds International – the multi-million pound erotic-shed company I set up last year, after my wife left me. Or I'm a brass-plate engraver. No, the first one.

So whoever kidnapped me must be after a ransom! Unless . . . I shudder as I suddenly realize what it is I can smell – Chanel N°5. But why would a woman want to tie me up like this? As hard as I try, with my pounding head, I can't think of any woman I've upset. Disappointed? Plenty. But upset?

As my memory slowly returns, I see a young man. Me. And a shed. My shed. And a woman. Several women, in fact . . .

'So,' I asked eagerly, 'Do you like the feel of a feather on your naked skin?'

'I'm not sure,' she said, 'Maybe if you took it off the pigeon first?'

I was worried my leaky shed
might ruin our night of passion
but luckily I managed to get felt up
on the roof.

She lay naked on my workbench with just a carrot, a lettuce and a cauliflower covering her nether regions. She called it a vegazzle.

She said she wanted us to try
tea bagging but I just couldn't do
it. I only keep Nescafé in the shed.

My tongue flicked in and out, faster and faster until she was completely helpless. No woman can resist a good lizard impression.

'Give it to me now and give it to me hard!' she begged.

'Alright,' I said, 'But I still think a Viennetta's better when it's defrosted.'

'Make love to me like you've never made love to anyone before!' she pleaded.

'Okay,' I said, putting on my penguin costume.

She told me she was turned on
by dangerous men, so I started
running with scissors.

'Not there . . . there!'
she yelled, banging
the workbench with
her fist. 'Oh yes . . .
yes . . . YES!'

She took *Where's
Wally?* very seriously.

She told me to wait in the shed –
she wanted to try a bit of role play.
The black leather didn't worry me.
Or the heavy breathing. But I was a
bit concerned when she said, 'Luke,
I am your father.'

'Open your mouth,' I ordered, tying the blindfold over her eyes. Before long, I was completely satisfied. She definitely couldn't tell Coke from Pepsi.

'Take me roughly on your multi-purpose workbench again,' she begged. I smiled. It's true what they say – once you go Black & Decker, you never go back.

After that weekend in the shed, I never saw her again. It turned out she wasn't looking for a relationship, she was just DIY-curious.

Now I see my face behind the windscreen of a beige Ford Focus, cheeks as damp as my shed. My quest for garden-based love having proved fruitless, I'd turned, disillusioned and despondent, to the countless possibilities of the internet, the open road . . . and houses . . .

'Get down on your hands and knees and I'll take you to a place you've never been before.'

I obeyed, nervously.

This was the strictest satnav ever.

'I'm so hot and wet I can hardly stand it,' she moaned.

'I know,' I said; 'It must be tough going through the menopause in Wales.'

She told me she was turned on by men who took risks – so I took the plastic off the sofa.

Our first session wasn't a great success. I asked her to come as Miss Whiplash so she turned up with a neck brace and a solicitor.

She wanted to try phone sex so I pretended to be an IT support guy. It turned her on at first. Then it turned her off again.

'Mmmm, that's it,' she moaned,
'Now pinch it between your fingers,
wiggle it about then pull gently.'

I was only too happy to follow
her instructions. I'd never played
Jenga before.

She told me she was
into extreme bondage
– so I took her to see
Skyfall six times.

As we sat in the dark restaurant, she stroked my thigh and whispered seductively into my ear, 'I want to see your hardness.'

'Alright,' I replied, and punched the waiter.

At the touch of her lips, it grew long and swollen. I gasped as she squeezed and pulled expertly. It was the best balloon giraffe I'd ever seen.

I met many women, but one thing soon became clear – being a long-distance Lothario wasn't for me. I was too far out of my comfort zone – my shed. I rack my brains but I just can't think why any of those women might want to kidnap me. An overwhelming sense of hopelessness begins to seep through me when, for some reason, another face flashes across my mind. Of course – Brenda! If anyone would want to tie me up and torture me, it's her. Our marriage had started off well enough – at least, before she read THAT book. I sigh as I recall that first, magical year – the thrill of moving into our first house, our first summer together, our first Christmas . . .

'Is that good?' I asked.

'Mmmm . . . yes,' she murmured.

'And that?'

'Oh yes!' she squealed.

'And that?'

'Oh God, yes!!' she cried.

I sighed. At this rate we'd never choose a new sofa.

'You're making me so hot,' she
breathed.

'I know,' I said. 'Maybe the shed
wasn't the best place for a barbecue.'

She slowly ran each ice cube over the tip of my manhood. It was a sensual and erotic ritual – but it did mean our guests had to wait a bit longer for their drinks.

As I lay beneath a sea of
writhing limbs, exploring
and grasping hungrily,
I realized something.
I hated Christmas shopping.

'I've been a very naughty girl,' she said, licking her lips. 'I need to be punished.' So I bought her the Daniel O'Donnell Christmas album.

I lay helpless on the shed floor, my hands tied and my mouth covered with tape. I never could get the hang of wrapping presents.

She sighed as my right hand
moved slowly in and out and gasped
as I thrust it in one more time.

It isn't easy doing the Hokey Cokey
in a shed.

Our marriage continued nicely and before long we reached that comfortable stage – the one after the early, uncomfortable stage and before the later, extremely painful stage . . .

'Mmmm . . . that's so good,' she sighed, 'You know just how I like it.'

'Of course I do,' I grinned, 'Milk, two sugars.'

Each firm stroke was bringing me closer and closer to that moment of relief and satisfaction. Soon my shed would be completely weatherproof.

'Do it!' she begged, desperately.

'Okay,' I said, tying her hands and fastening the gag over her mouth, 'But there must be easier ways to give up chocolate.'

As soon as she entered the shed, I could see that burning look in her eyes that meant just one thing. Her conjunctivitis had flared up again.

'I'm so wet,' she purred, 'You know what to do . . .'

I certainly did. I went straight to B&Q and got a dehumidifier for the shed.

I love stacking my barbecues in my shed at the end of summer. You can't beat a bit of grill-on-grill action.

She said she wanted me to be more romantic so I gave her a massage with essential oils – Castrol GTX and WD-40.

Bondage is so much easier now we're older. I used to have to blindfold her, now I just hide her glasses.

She said it turned her on to watch me
pleasure myself. So I cracked open a
beer and watched *Match of the Day*.

But eventually, inevitably, after several years of married bliss, things took a downward turn and we began to take each other for granted . . .

She looked up through her fringe and whispered, 'Tonight, you are my master and I am your slave. Your wish is my command . . .'

So I got her to clear out the shed.

'I want it now. Against this wall!' she demanded. 'And keep it up as long as possible.'

'Don't worry,' I said, 'I know how to put up a shelf.'

I stood there, staring coldly down at her naked, bound body for several minutes before finally leaving in silence. Don't you hate it when you go into the shed for something and you can't remember what?

Her body tensed and quivered as she
felt wave after wave surge through it.

I probably should have told her about
the new electric fence.

I inserted it gently and began to wiggle it – slowly at first, then with increasing urgency.

She began to moan.

'When are you going to get a new key for that shed door?'

'Prepare to suffer like no other man has,' she said, drawing her razor-sharp fingernail up the cellophane of the *Sex and the City* box set.

'Use me,' she whispered, moistening her lips with her tongue.

'Very well,' I said, 'Hold the ladder while I creosote the shed roof.'

'This time, really hurt me,' she begged, pressing her body up against the shed wall.

'Alright,' I said, 'You're a terrible cook and I fancy your sister.'

'I'm your slave,' she said, breathlessly, 'Make me feel completely helpless and worthless.'

So I locked her in the shed and went to the pub.

My brow furrows. My marriage to Brenda hadn't been perfect but I'd always been faithful – after all, why go out for a conservatory when you've got a shed at home? Why would she do this to me? Suddenly another image ripples into view. A woman outside my office. My mind's eye tries to focus on her face as she reaches into her purse and pulls out . . . a blindfold! And everything goes dark . . .

'So, you're awake.'

My mind jumps sharply back to the present. I'm no longer alone.

'Finally.'

I freeze. The voice is firm and precise – a voice I haven't heard since I was a naive, inexperienced young gardener at Mellors Manor . . . Ah, Lady Christina . . .

'Mmmm . . . that's so good, don't stop!' cried Lady Christina as I took careful aim and sprayed thoroughly. She always enjoyed it when I stimulated her clematis.

I found her lying naked on the shed floor, covered only in rose petals.

'So,' she purred, 'What do you think?'

I blinked. 'I'm not sure. Could be greenfly?'

Her fingers ran up and down its length until finally it spurted all over her heaving bosom. She'd clearly never used a watering can before.

Staring at her naked body leaning over my workbench, I asked what she wanted. She told me to go for something between a smack and a stroke. So I went for a smoke.

'Don't hold back,' she said, bending over in the middle of the lawn. 'Give it all you've got.' I didn't need telling twice – I hadn't played leapfrog in years.

Being tied to a large wooden cross wearing only a leather thong felt a bit strange at first. But it certainly kept the crows away from my cabbages.

'Stick it right up there,' she said. 'I want to remember this!' I did, then I patted it firmly. You can't be too careful with Post-it notes.

'So,' she asked curiously, 'How do you feel about being in chains?'

'It depends,' I replied, 'Nando's is okay but I'm not so keen on McDonald's.'

She was such a tease.
'I'm just going to slip into
something hot and see-
through,' she promised.

I waited all night in that
greenhouse . . .

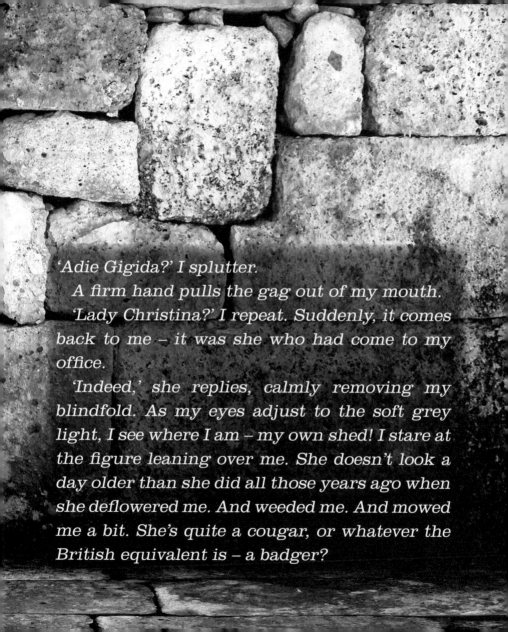

'Adie Gigida?' I splutter.

A firm hand pulls the gag out of my mouth.

'Lady Christina?' I repeat. Suddenly, it comes back to me – it was she who had come to my office.

'Indeed,' she replies, calmly removing my blindfold. As my eyes adjust to the soft grey light, I see where I am – my own shed! I stare at the figure leaning over me. She doesn't look a day older than she did all those years ago when she deflowered me. And weeded me. And mowed me a bit. She's quite a cougar, or whatever the British equivalent is – a badger?

'You haven't changed a bit,' I say, my bloodshot eyes tracing her every curve.

'On the contrary,' she says coolly, a wistful smile playing over her full lips, 'I've changed lots of bits. That's the beauty of being married to a cosmetic surgeon.'

'I . . . thought Lord Mellors was an explorer?'

'Oh he was,' she says, pensively. 'He was a true pioneer. He took liposuction to the Amazon basin, Botox to Guatemala . . . and pretty much everything to Essex.'

'Was?'

Her voice lowered.

'I just came from his funeral. That's why I'm wearing black.'

'I see,' I say, eyeing her long black gloves, thigh-length boots and leather basque. 'So you kidnapped me for my money. Couldn't you just have asked?'

'Don't be so vulgar,' Lady Christina replies, indignant. 'And ridiculous. I've never kidnapped anyone. My husband took very good care of me. Financially, at any rate . . .'

'Then why did you drug me?'

'Drug you?' she laughs. 'Don't you remember? After I blindfolded you – purely in the spirit of friendship, of course – you banged your head on your office door. Right on that silly brass plate. I offered to take you to A&E but you said you just wanted to be here in your shed. You're terribly cute when you're concussed.'

'So why am I bound and gagged?'

Lady Christina sucks her lip, coyly.

'Old habits die hard . . .'

'And the water torture?'

'Your roof. It leaks.'

I look up and feel a sudden rush of guilt as I realize I've neglected my one true love – my shed.

'I saw this and came to congratulate my dear little Colin,' says Lady Christina, unrolling a magazine. There I am on the cover, standing in front of the giant, award-winning ErotiShed 3000 – complete with sauna, stocks and optional Wi-Fi. 'So,' she continues, kneeling down and placing a gloved hand on my knee. 'I see you've made it . . . big.'

'I suppose so,' I say nervously. Shed designers don't like to boast but I have to admit it wasn't the first time I'd had to get planning permission for one of my erections. I bite my lip as her fingers walk slowly up my thigh. My inner gardener has grabbed a can of cider and is dancing Gangnam style.

Suddenly, the shed door flies open. A sodden figure stands silhouetted against the grey sky.

'Brenda?' I cry. 'What are you doing here? Er, meet . . . an old friend of mine, Lady Christina Mellors. I used to . . . tend her garden.'

'Charmed,' says Lady Christina, offering one hand while keeping the other firmly on my lap.

Brenda stands motionless, fixing my former employer with a steely glare.

'Well that was obviously a very long time ago. I think you'll find he's been tending my garden far more recently!'

'Really?' says Lady Christina, coolly looking Brenda up and down, 'I'd say it was more of a hanging basket.'

'So . . . this is nice,' I say, as nonchalantly as I can, handcuffed and bound to a chair. 'Why don't you come in? It's pouring.'

'Is it raining?' Brenda growls through gritted teeth. 'I hadn't noticed.'

I shuffle awkwardly, acutely aware of the proximity of Lady Christina's thumb to my nether regions.

'So, er, what brings you here? Today? Of all days?'

'I came to bring you these,' she begins, drawing a large brown envelope from her handbag, 'To sign. Our divorce papers. I thought it was time to move on finally . . .' She pauses, looking me up and down. ' . . . But now I'm not so sure. Maybe I made a terrible mistake leaving you.' She slowly places the envelope back into her bag and takes a step forward. 'I'm just a girl, standing in front of a boy, asking him to bend her over his workbench, smear her buttocks with Swarfega and spank her till Whitsuntide.'

Staring at the dripping figure before me, a warm sensation fills my chest.

'Now wait a minute . . .'

My eyes return to the woman with her hand on my groin.

'You may not have moved on but your husband clearly has,' declares Lady Christina. 'Now, off you go, dear girl – and don't let the door hit you on that rather ample posterior on the way out.'

'That's it!' says Brenda, tossing her handbag onto the shed floor. 'Let's sort this out, right now!'

'Very well,' responds Lady Christina, calmly removing her gloves.

I hold my breath, horrified – they're actually going to fight over me!

'Ladies, don't!' I plead. 'This is wrong!'

They pause, fists raised, and turn to look at me.

'Not in the shed. Go into the garden.'

I crane my neck to peer through the shed window as the two most important women in my life square furiously up to one another. Before long they're on the ground, wrestling fiercely in the mud – clawing, biting and yanking. I gulp excitedly as I stare wide-eyed at the scene before me. The vegetable patch has never looked better.

After an hour of hot, wet, muddy, girl-on-girl action they – and I – are spent. Brenda and Lady Christina stagger wearily back into the shed.

'It's no good,' they say, in unison. 'You're going to have to choose.'

I gaze dumbly at them both. I don't know what to say. I'm just a simple man. All I know is I like my women like I like my sheds – warm, accommodating and slightly warped. I have an impossible choice to make.

Or do I?

Maybe, just maybe, there's another solution.

Unconventional, perhaps. Risky, almost certainly. But a solution nonetheless.

Very slowly, the corners of my mouth begin to turn upwards . . .

Two's company but . . . three in a shed?

Picture Acknowledgements

Page 14 © Kaz Chiba/Getty Images, 36 © Kevin Allan/Getty Images, 38 and 39 © Inti St. Clair/Getty Images, 90 © Tim Platt/Getty Images, 140 and 141 © moodboard/Getty Images.

The following images are used under licence from Shutterstock.com, 2013:

Page 6 © Veniamin Kraskov, 8 and 9 © Valentin Agapov, 10 © Rigucci, 13 © █████, 16 and 17 © daffodilred, 18 © terekhov igor, 21 © Andrew Haddon, 22 © Ivan Bondarenko, 25 © perlphoto, 27 © OlgaLis, 28 and 29 © █████, 31 © Katie Smith Photography, 32 © Jason Vandehey, 35 © Simaa █████, 40 and 41 © Brykaylo Yuriy, 42 and 43 © Ryan Jorgensen – Jo███, 44 © Andrew Haddon, 47 © UgputuLf SS, 48 © PRILL, 51 © Ma█████ Kar██, and 53 © Chrislofotos, 55 © Leshik, 56 © drKaczmar, 58 and 59 █████, 60 © pulsar75, 63 © igor.stevanovic, 64 © stocknadia, 66 and 67 © Green████, 68 © Maria Dryfhout, 71 © lehvis, 72 © Pete Spiro, 74 and 75 © De██ Georgiev, 76 © debr22pics, 79 © Dushenina, 80 and 81 © Estai███ Andreas Schalber, 85 © Gillian Entress, 86 © █████ and 89 © Graeme Dawes, 93 © KAppleyard, 94 © Gr████pa █████ d Boord, 98 © Graeme Dawes, 100 and 101 © Christian Colis██ █████ ███hs, 105 © Lena Lir, 106 © c.byatt-norman, 109 © Mich███ ████ © Tom Gowanlock, 112 and 113 © Todd Klassy, 114 © Chri███ ███ ██ 117 © Fedor A. Sidorov, 118 © Gudrun Muenz, 121 © Sun█ █████ 1█2 © Brendan Howard, 124 and 125 © Nanisimova, 126 © Hum████ ███ © George Burba, 130 © svic, 132 and 133 © Gemenacom, 134 █████ ████esart, 136 © Todd Klassy, 138 and 139 © Repina Valeriya, 142 █████ ██cher.